*This book is dedicated to
Eric Alder*

Bread Widow

A Book of Poetry

emmett wheatfall

Reflections Publishing House
Inglewood, CA

ewheatfall@gmail.com
P.O. Box 30105
Portland, OR 97294

Cover Design by – Clark Graphics

ISBN 978-0-9837231-8-9
Library of Congress Control Number 2013943685
First Printing,   July 2013

Printed in the United States of America

www.reflectionspublishings.net

Contents

FOREWORD

I am sitting here on a dreary, gray afternoon, when Mother Nature has found herself caught between the seasons, not sure whether she's quite ready to trade in what has been a fierce and wintry spring, for our much more gentle summer. And while I find myself tired of damp, there is no denying there is no better type of afternoon than reading poetry written by poet emmett wheatfall.

Over the past two years, I must confess, I have fallen head over heels for this poet who has broadened my horizons, brought me comfort on difficult days, and has inspired my own pen, making me want to be a better writer. In this world of a digitized, instant, self-published plethora of poetry, there is no higher compliment I can pay. emmett wheatfall is a fresh, honest, and most importantly, very wise voice in the ever growing chorus, where mining the true gems grows even more difficult.

This seasoned poet is not only the creator of a library of poetic work, spoken word, and smooth jazz styling's, but he is also an amazing champion for poetry and its survival.

We are alive, reading and word-seeding during an amazing time of connection. A time where we can reach with our invisible hands into the ether, connecting with those who inspire and motivate. I am so very blessed to have connected with emmett, so wonderfully surprised to engage in an ever running and evolving conversation in regards to the status of poetry today, and our purpose here, exploring what we can do to promote and lift up this amazing art form called poetry. The fact you're reading this, tells me, you're willing to help.

I invite you now into emmett's fourth collection. As a resident fan and reader first, I've enjoyed watching emmett's pen not

8

only grow and evolve, but the expanding faith in his own pen to where he writes with such authority and purpose, a splendid confidence I hope to one day have. It's a journey I highly recommend...as it's the growth of a writer displayed beautifully and without fear for the world to see.

If you are a first time reader of emmett's work, please know you are starting with what is a fantastic and incredible collection. His path is peppered with a smart humor, bringing a smile on the heels of a tear, illuminating the heart, lyrical song, faith, and as evidenced in all his work an incredibly keen and discerning eye towards man and his nature.

I could easily list my favorites, but you dear reader, would rush to them, thus losing the magic of the journey. "Bread Widow" is a wonderfully wise collection from one of our most vibrant contemporary poets. Trust me; by reading these words you've played a vital role in pushing poetry forward. Just as emmett does every time he reaches for his number 2 pencil.

I've certainly stolen enough time from your reading moments, and evening has fallen here now. It's time for me to try to "catch a glimpse of the stars" through the clouds that still linger and ponder *Our Meaning of Life*. Like the *Number 2 Pencil* emmett speaks of, there are times we have to drop the pencil and see to saving ourselves. This collection just might help us do that.

Natasha Head

Natasha Head is a published poet who hails from the beautiful east coast of Canada. You can find her work in Inspiration Speaks Volume 1, and her debut collection, 2012 Pushcart Prize nominated Nothing Left to Lose, both available through Winter Goose Publishing. Her blog, tashtoo.com, is a vibrant example of her work in progress. She is also a proud OpenLinkNight host and resident tweeter for dVersePoets, and founding member of The New World Creative Union. Join her on BlogTalkRadio's The Creative Nexus each Thursday.

13 Knots With A Noose

His hat—tin foil
Necktie—13 knots with a noose
A straightened coat hanger—his cane
He thinks I look weird

His coat—a Hefty Trash Bag
Shirt—bare chest
A faded denim from Goodwill—his pant
I utter not a word

His socks—crusty brown wool
Shoes—without soles
A pair of eyeglasses—lensless
Our world turns

Him—a fashion magnet—

for the homeless. Me—the social

conformist.

1642 To 1649

Seething has never been sanguine
On occasion I'm told moons have
Ruddy the seething my eyes of blood
Having read Nathaniel Hawthorne's
The scarlet Letter
Hester Prynne don't you cry don't you cry
So repugnant the indignity you find
On scaffolding made of scorn
Bleed red my seething eyes of soul
Dead to you your husband of youth
Presumed lost at sea somewhere
Your bed did another man warm
Between legs your thighs he's worn
Now the scarlet letter A you wear
Hester Prynne don't you cry don't you cry
You modern woman you
So repugnant the indignity you find

24 Roses

William Stafford said
Follow the golden thread
So
We give ourselves to reason
Weave ourselves anew
And the bloom shall come
Twice the dozen roses

* In loving memory of Oregon Poet Laureate William Stafford.

A Golden Diadem

With the letter _m_ my missive ends.

When his Saintly saints shall marvel,
each in their own astonishment, and,
Jesus Is My Savior sings the angelic
choir; a single sparrow shall flutter
overhead, with olive branches in its
mouth; Jesus shall seat himself on
the throne of God, never taking his
eyes off the sparrow, until, everyone,
has adorned themselves by placing
upon their head—

a golden diade_m_.

A Perfect Night

...like a drip that breaks the silence
of a perfect night. ~ Melvin Eldridge

Too soon. It's yet to be morning. A
Millstone anchors you lest you rise—
Lest you rise, too soon.

You dream. Open is the doorway door.
There is no light. Somewhere beyond
The darkness is silence—you dream.

A perfect night. Only for a drip,
That breaks the silence will you rise,
In this—a perfect night.

A Rose In A Pocket

I have never noticed a rose
in a woman's pocket—until
today, and will never again,
with pen in all my days quill.

Adopt A Child

All the mangos are ready
Smiling to their hearts delight
Resting in big bamboo baskets
Mango lovers will pick them
Take them to big new homes
Wash them thoroughly until clean
Put them in big bowls of their own
Where everyone will see them
On big coffee tables in living rooms
Some will be carried in big baskets
To the park where they'll entertain
They'll be objects of big delight
Only to return before sundown
To big bowls that are their own
Where everyone will see them
Smiling to their hearts delight

African Moon

I heard your heart break
Scattering glass everywhere
Shattering unspoken sentiment
As is the usual way it begins
Before the bleeding
The uncontrollable bleeding
Seeping through the cracks
Of your veneer
That tapa cloth tissue
Being thinly veiled scrim
Of feminine emotion
I loved so much

Ain't To Proud To Beg

There is no taste in my mouth
My libido I constantly douse
This mind of mine tends to make-believe
When I pee it's like parting the Red China Sea
I'm like a ship without a signet for its sail
A smoke jumper sporting a contrail
Still
I ain't too proud to beg

Even though I can't skip across the floor
It's factual my hair just won't grow anymore
Children hide when they catch eye of me
Not a word I say do old people believe
I sit and watch lots of cars go bye
Not long from now I'll being saying goodbye
Still
I ain't too proud to beg

Are Women Worthy

Are women on earth and among men worthy of valor,
the vigor required by honor, virile in the potency of triumph?
Can she wield the blade made of steel with the swift retribution
of an angry god? Will her breasts, let lay abreast her breasts,
the breastplate of leather righteousness with all its signatures
and symbols? With what must her loins be girded? A chastity belt?
And her painted toes, with their circular signets, signs of
the number of times tested for admittance into the legion! Can
she war with the fiercest of warrior men? Can she keep rank
at the moment of imminent breach? Or will she cower the way of
cows before slaughter? Honor is to the victor not the vanquished,
not the female nor the male, but the triumphant. Are women
worthy of valor, the vigor required by honor? Are they?

At Its End

To shine today the sun said yes
Stormy clouds appeared anyway
Rain did fall upon this the earth
At its end it was okay but
Of new the day draws near a dawn
With a selfless sense of its worth

Before We Cry

Men, we die
We die more when
A woman soldier dies
We wince inside
We cry inside
No woman should die
In battle
Before we cry
Women, we cry
We die more when
A woman soldier dies
We can't lie

Blossom Blue

Wistful love, from once,
a backward blossom; blue,
now, a reddish plum.

Boston

Ah!
The sky is so Boston today.

I speak English,
when I want too.

Play Spades with you?
Wearing Bostonians?

Run a Boston on you?
All 13 tricks?

But you won't let me;
you won't let me.

When I want too,
I speak English.

Yes!
So Boston is the sky today.

Bread Widow

he died at dinner
ready was the bread
weeping she wept
while hungry
for leavened bread
his unleavened life

Character Content

Half empty?

Hello.
What's your name?
Malcom, Mookie, Markus, Morris?
But of course, what's in a name?
Thug, Hood
N-word, boy

THE GLASS

Hello.
What's your name?
William, Walter, Winston, Wesley?
Of course, but what's in a name?
Sir William, Lord Walter
President Winston, Mr. Wesley

Half full?

Choo Choo

To pen a farewell is deliberate if a pen is available.
Without it the goodbye is undiscoverable and irretrievable.
So sing goodbye to the tune of a lullaby. Choose to coo.
Shoo away the naysayers when you encounter the
Choo Choo train circling the baby's crib before you go.

It's a long way from the Western front, where it's quiet.
You'll get there though, by Choo Choo too. It will huff and puff;
Toot tooting its way on the train track. So pen that farewell.
And always remember; keep a pen in your pocket.
Without it the goodbye is undiscoverable and irretrievable.

Christ The Poet King

I was hungry,
And you gave me
No verse.

I was thirsty,
And you said nothing
To inspire me.

I was a stranger,
And not a *spoken-word*
You spoke.

I was naked,
And you clothed me not
With prosody.

I was sick,
And you visited me
With enjambments.

I was in prison,
And the revelation of you
Appeared to me.

Cognitive Dissonance

Away again I take flight
      As if advertisement for lift
No. It's just my imagination
      Confronting something greater
That cognitive dissonance
      Between reality and fear
Fact opposing assurance
      Myth transcending legend
When reality sets in again
      Then,
      I change the channel

Come September

Come September
Come go away with me
Lay not to count each day
Like rosé petals though they fade
Through passing of night
Unto dawn of new morning
Until mourning comes
Come September
Come go away with me

Crass Comments

How crass the comments
When a picture is worth its weight
In oil

A canvass does not lie
Even though speechless
It still speaks

So refined the strokes
Partial and parting fits of anger
Laced in tender brushing

Will there be a buyer
Of its sentiment
If ever the sentimental

Galleries accept visitors
Silence an unwritten rule
Still crass the comments

Dilemma

I don't need a writing prompt.
What pompous ass suggests that?

Is it one by day; two, if by night?

There is a whiff of powder in the air.

Is that not enough to write?

Fat Back Jazz Guitar

Why would she want to run if she could hop, skip, and jump?
Unshackle her feet and let her dance. She's tired of looking inside out.
If you let her she'll sing the last stanza of your song.

Play that fat back jazz guitar Mr. jazz man.

Give her a reason and she'll love you. Your name will be her name:
Your frame of mind her mind. Move over and she'll fill your void.
She'll silence your proclivities. Give her a reason to love you.

Folly

The broken plate,
where fasting lasts,
suggests hunger.

A faceless picture
is in frame,
as empty reminder
of what was, and will never
be again.

Sinners of all souls
are lost,
their path to redemption
runs through perdition.

Not everything staid
is explicable,
something the illiterate find
inexplicable.

It is the fool's folly,
who fails to understand

the broken plate.

Give Wink To Twinkling Stars

Less death is not so much
A cent the penny of its existence
Rub two together
Then note the value change
Mercy—irrelevant
Justice—fleeting satisfaction
Salvation—tomorrow's hope for today
Cash-in the morning's awakening
Spend-thrift the multifaceted day
Give bow to the bow of night
Give wink to twinkling stars
Sleep only to give rise to the new day
Live life luminous and sleep like you've lived
Less death is not so much
A cent the penny of its existence

Golden Brown

O, this the beautiful day.
Kiss me O you the sun,
Kiss me all day long.
Keep me golden brown,
And kiss me all the day long.

Hail To Thee

I sit among the plumb apple trees
Pleasured by their fruit-bearing seed
Relieved of minions from failures past
I for now sit unmasked

Seed me as if the unborn reed
For soon I'll gaze a schooner on the sea
Engulfed in wind its bleach white scrim
Hail to thee O' seafaring friend

Her

Some claim...

To have come from Him
Others, to speak for Him
And one, to be Him

But all of them
Came from—
her

High Wire

At first I took you for a bird. Then I
Mistook you for a squirrel, in the tree
Adjacent my driveway, only to discover
Upon investigation, you were a bird
Making all that noise, making all that noise,
Perched, and alone, on that exceedingly
High wire, after having juxtaposed yourself,
Perpendicular to the one before I arrived
To take note of you, you proceed to take
A huge crap above me you little bastard.
The nerve of you a fowl of the air,
You fowl feathered creature of flight,
You flatulent farce from firmament. And,
Then to take flight to another exceedingly
High wire? You little bastard you. *You*
Little bastard you!

Him Or Her?

I fell in love once
By never doing so again
Having stumbled upon a step
Beneath my field of vision
Ensuing my loss of balance
Given the gravity of the occasion
Unequal the distribution of equity
My heart filled with despair
He caught me
As if a scripted moment
In the midst of my free-fall
Here is what I know
Ordained by embrace
I fell in love once

Hugo

A man died today, as all men do. His name—
Hugo. His parting words were

Please, don't let me die.

To some in the *West*, a dictator. In Venezuela—
El Presidente. To his daughters and son *papi*.

There are those who rejoice, and those
who weep, and them that don't give a damn.

But they too shall die one day, as all mankind
must do. Like the birds that fall from the sky,

when in their last flight, having fulfilled
their destiny.

Hugo,

fought for his life, fought the good fight, having
now taken anew,

a new place,

a new journey.

Hopefully, he has now turned his sword into
a plowshare, his rhetoric, to rebel rousing peace;

and to never again ask—

Please, don't let me die.

I Forgive You

I cannot entrust to you
the world to come,
for you are not like me
in most all your ways.

You are irreverent,
ill-tempered,
self-centered.
You are inconsiderate of others,
self-righteous,
believe inordinately
in your own ordinances.

You fail to consider my wisdom,
which is the wisdom of ages,
the loftiness of my understanding,
the immutability
of my righteous judgment,
the limitless scope
of my provincial authority.

If only you could wish to be me.

Do you think yourself to be a god?
If so—

I forgive you.

I Have Never Kissed A Man

I have never kissed a man
On his mouth with my mouth
Commingling my breath with his
Teasing his tongue with mine

Romantic as this may sound
It is not so for me
It does mean something to him
It is not so for me

I am heterosexual
He is homosexual

He has not kissed a woman
On her mouth with his mouth
Commingling his breath with hers
Teasing her tongue with his

Romantic as this may sound
It is not so for him
It does mean something to me
It is not so for him

I have never kissed a man

I Knew You Would Come

In bed with me is poetry.
I am naked; she is not.

She says

I have waited for you
I knew you would come
Begin again
What you have begun before
What you will finish again

I—am yours

It's morning. She is naked.
And I—clothed in poetry.

I Think I Knew

I am never the man I would be
Neither are the men I think I knew

Lest We Forget

Mounted on Rushmore are faces,

Etched in stone, chiseled by hands made of zeal.

But who cares?
These stone face men,

Testaments to the tenacity of their conviction,

Decay daily,
Like flesh and bone, unlike

Their lasting legacies, as recorded in the annuals

Of distant time, dispensation,
And circumstance. The rain has come,

And shall continue falling, washing the force of fate

Off their faces,
Lest we forget, that these were mere men—

Not our fathers, not gods, not immortal, but men,

Mere men.

Life In The Well

This soul lost in serendipity is ghostly. Translucent
are dried tears. Soon this rose will blossom. Some things
beautiful take time. There is life in the well of one's
own darkness. I shudder to think it. Whoever pulls me
up from the deep—I see you.

Looniness

If Raisin Bread became the toast of town,
and paraded itself through the streets on a float,
I'd shake my finger at it with great distain, knowing
you never float Raisin Bread through the streets,
but on a plate, while Wile E. Coyote and Road Runner
go at it, in the tradition most notable in the looniness
of Looney Tunes, aired on a T.V., with rabbit ears
made from wire coat hangers, retrieved from closets
where all the clothes lay on the floor, awaiting the new
coat hangers that will never come, because ACME
is not a real company, and the milk on the coffee table,
in front of the T.V., will turn lukewarm if not consumed
in the spirit of laughter brought on by looniness.

Love Song By The Sea

I will sing me a love song,
by the sea, where it woos me,
the song I sing, woos me.

The sea, she knows me. Who
would know otherwise, till I sing
me a love song, by the sea.

A seagull sings with me, my
love song, beneath the clouds
she sings, by the sea.

The tiny sea urchin makes us
three, by the sea; living on the
surface of light the breeze.

We woo me, the song we sing.
The love song I sing, down by
the sea; woos me.

Lowly Gods

Look not
to resurrection,
wherein you believe;
but to ascension,
to lowly gods,
poetic gods.

Nevertheless
exalted; they
are familial.

Look to be one.
Only one;
a poetry god,
among the gods,
gods of poetry.

Be one.

Modern ~ X

I wrote a sealed muse with my own pen, having issued it not
within the court of poetic opinion, but my own sense of self-
indulgence, which is not without warrant, but a terrible anvil
of such self-virulence and tangential sense of pride for a man
fully seduced by the inflated dictates of abhorrent envy. I just
had to write such a muse on brown paper with my own pen.
[Caesura]
It's sealed now. I've put my pen down. Never will jurors of my
poetic peers unseal my muse for the purpose of scansion.

Modern ~ X

Never Mind That

I've been to Hell.
You wouldn't know it
unless I told you. I
dug it up. Never mind
that. It's cold here.
What love was
is now no more. Is
Cupid's quiver empty?
I won't quibble over
it. I, won't quibble.
It's, so, cold here.

Night Praise

With this beginning,
I see day's end.

Rising through me
is sweet, this a night's
praise.

From these my lips,
lisping, listing, with

heavy eyes, my
light heart; I whisper
saying,

"I love you Lord, I
 do. I'm carried away,

by the melodies,
the majesty, of this
a night's praise."

"Carry me. Carry me,
to the new day."

Number 2 Pencil

Can the literalist become the literary, or the pauper a proper, even the feral domesticated? Is there a need to reconcile these? Are they congruent, symmetrical, quizzical? Should argument arise, put down the number 2 pencil; walk away:

Save yourself.

O But For Oceans

Each day on earth
Outpaces me,

And passing nights—
Far less enlightening.

O but for oceans
Here and there.

Rolling me in,
Splaying me out.

Must I look down,
And swear before Sedna:

I was blind once,
But I see now.

Our Meaning Of Life

At the beginning there were these stars
these little moons with their own big earth
and tiny sun clamoring for man to come from
where they've come and give them meaning
not in the mean way he's come killing
and wars followed by wars ethnic cleansing
religious division separating him like the
neighboring galaxies he cannot number in
the sophistication of his finite sanctimonious
knowledge and knowability because
his free-will has made him selfish and evil
choking out what is good making good appear
beautiful although seldom seen something
accentuated in the moment of its actualization
rendering good coveted in the eyes of its
beholder whose been made weary by the
death and destruction pushing him to rush into
the midnight of night looking for the perfect
moment to catch a glimpse of these stars
who were at the beginning before him so that
he might find his own sense of meaning

Poor Creatures

I came to the conclusion; I could not come to one, at
the end of an argument as it were, with its intersections
overlapping like stitches in a knitted garment. If only
my feelings stopped getting in the way, the way a
kitten does in the kitchen when looking for fresh milk,
or the spider's spun web that's unseen, meshed
together over time, left to harbor the poor creatures
who souls have recently departed because of a fatal
act of domestic violence, spurred on by that age old
doctrine called *Predestination*, formulated in the best
European minds of those called theologians, from places
like Germany, Sweden, France, and England I guess.
I still have not come to a conclusion on that matter.

Pretentious

A phlox petal lies powerless;
as if speechless the mute spoke;
only once.

Of her virtue,
what glory is there?

A fetid genus. Wilted pink;
once potent. Pretentious this the
phlox petal.
Of her virtue,
what glory is there?

Purple Lips

Pilfered kisses from purple lips
Rouge so rosy the roses blush
Limn so light it looks lovely

Succulent these tender teasing
Stolen in several seconds of kissing
Where 'no' never means 'no'

And yes

The burning essence
Of
Pilfered kisses from purple lips

Redemption

I walked chalked lines
Until rain washed them away
All the while
Prayer after prayer
Evaporated like morning dew
Until I plucked
A four-leaf clover
And that rainbow appeared

Then I cried

Revolution

Of revolution there was once talk,
boisterous talk, by ignorant braggarts
romancing revolution, who knew nothing

of bloodshed,

of torn flesh and limb,

of disfigurement and death.

The more they bragged
the more boisterous they became.
They are the romantically inclined,
whose imagination glorifies

the rockets' red glare,

the bombs bursting in air,

the slicing with bayonet mounted knives,

the hand over a mouth

that snuffs out a life in these the eyes

of the romantically inclined.

Fools romanticize revolution, but I say
"Just kill them all!"

Second Fiddle

I gazed upon the distant face of the moon tonight
Just before some dark clouds started a peep show
Leading me to question the validity of my encounter
With that high-minded yellow bastard who plays
Second fiddle to the sun in the backyard of space

I know why mankind never went back to the moon
Even why we left his place so littered with junk
A space mobile that is no longer salvageable
Packets of orange flavored Tang and the U.S. flag
Which use to satisfy our big thirst for patriotism

So instead of feeling sorry for my unfortunate night
I summoned my wife from her impending slumber
Whereupon I gazed into the beauty of her face
With the noble-minded intent to tell her I love her
When my noisy neighbor who plays second fiddle

Came knocking at my door

Sequestration

theoretically he sliced his finger on a thought
souring him as if a sewer backing up unbeknown
to the grand bargain being struck by a rationale
wherein chess pieces on a checkered board
vie for position waiting to strike while compassion
reacquaints itself with loneliness as a much more
open state of nuanced misogyny litigates itself
upsetting balance of powers beset by the silent
sequestration of concerns found to be bleeding
in the content of faculty and the thrush of pain

Shoeless and Sweet

Shoeless newborn
Waterless ledge
Around the horn
Jagged cliff's edge

_____

Sweet baby's breath
Upright waterfall
Spiraling death
Unfortunate pitfall

_____

Sing Sing

His elocution electrifying
As the mocked mockingbird
By his own admission
Behind the bench of justice
Soon sentenced to Sing Sing
Where mockingbird men
Reside high on the high wire
In barb the wired bird cage

Six Syllables

Out of nothing I come.

Sticky Notes

Give earthly love
a new name; so
heavenly new moons

fail, flashing stars
flip flop like, Loch Ness
filled lies;

so sticky notes
lose their stickiness,
hems on skirts

unravel, revealing
certain unseemly sorts
of uncertainty—

then,

I'll slap myself
for such silliness of
poetic thought.

The Beauty Of Any Rose

I have never recited poetry in Latin
Decreed life sentences for poetic injustice
Scanned dictionaries for diction
Swore upon the King James Bible
Whispered prosody to myself
Called upon the wisdom of crowds
Cursed out loud W.S. Merwin's brilliance
Treated verse as impassioned dalliance
Succumbed to the beauty of any rose
Yielded the floor to nonsense
Aspired to anything less than greatness
Fawned over unbound paper books
Searched for love in the meaning of me
Boxed with God without gloves
Walked away wondering why
Been more inspired by the depth

Of these my words

The Leaves Do Rise

When again the leaves do rise,
I'll chase away their whining winds;
        for leaves know well my torment,
the torrent odium, cascading across
        the surface of my life.

The New Day

Everything is so kinetic
At all hours of everyday
Even past the midnight
That ushers in the new day
Without a bill of rights
Without a bill of sale
Rising from playful repose
Expanding upon horizons
Turning like tiny tumblers
As life itself goes on
Being the fantasy it is
As I pleasantly exhale

The Sad Sad World

There are trash mongers who troll
the depths of the marginalized.

When was the last time you
were regarded as marginalized? In
the pantheon of those piled high,
on the list of us having not escaped,
where do you rank?

It's unfortunate when the wind
is unable to blow us into oblivion.
What a sobering thought we share
with the slew.

If only the marginalized could run.
Of what is necessary to outpace
life's dump truck? Is the last vestige
of hope found in the refuge of all
trailer parks?

Such is the sad sad world.

This A Days' Dream

Upon the horizon must my eyes tend to their gaze
as I sit upon the glossy green mass of green grass
that rises, then falls; escalating as if an escalator
ferrying forward, then backward, beyond invisible
barriers of my infatuated imagination, whose had
nothing inebriating yet to augment its wonderment
as my eyes behold the rise of this a day's dream.

This New Morning

This new morning waits for me
As do the sheep in my small fold
Who rise to graze green grass
In the field that is my master's
Whose gone to visit his father
Whose houses I'm told are many
One of them is mine he says

My master is the Chief Shepherd
At least that's what I believe
As do the other shepherds I know
Whose folds are large and small
Whose sheep rise to graze grass
In the fields that are my master's
As this new morning awaits them

We Wove A Circle

We wove a circle
Made of vice and men
They succumbed
To continuance
Failed forbearance
To license
While we women
Watched and wept
Waiting for vindication
It did not come
The satisfaction
It did not come
A sense of salvation
Did not come
So we wove a circle
For ourselves

We've Been Lovers

Evening has come; I welcome it.
Now past is the light of day. I take
no thought of it; it of me. We've been

lovers for years. First came darkness,
then came light. I found darkness natural,

light artificial. If I were Shakespeare,
I would say "Darkness doth cometh;
light, thou art fleeting."

Am I the fool? Most certainly I am the
foolish. Darkness clings to me, covers
me, covets me, without economic cost.

Light feeds me, frees me, then flees me,
costing me something. Of what manner
is this? I know not. It's true, it's mine.
Evening has come; I welcome it.
Now past is the light of day; I take

no thought of it; it of me.

When Lunch Isn't Enough

Two fish,
five loaves of bread:

I'm still hungry
Jesus. I'm still,

hungry.

Who Weaves You?

So soft the sweet poet you are. Who weaves you with what?
What contemplations purge the dross of you? Whose ink
spills forth from foundation upon once a blank page? Is there
litmus for the license you take, teasing like talons from the
quill of your quips? I know of you. I'm nearer than the wisp
of wisdom laid light by slight of stroke, as if the brush of
tender blush applied faintly to concrete words. If spurned
by you I'll succumb, whereupon the page I'll gaze as the light
in my eyes dissipates, fading in the elegy of your soft words.
So soft the sweet poet you are, you are. Who weaves you?

Wind Ruffles Our Feathers

When wind ruffles our feathers
We have none and neither do you
Pretty and wide as they are
We wish to take flight as you do
But we are not clever enough
So we walk around angrily
With pretty wings spread wide
We have none and neither do you
When wind ruffles our feathers
We have none and neither do you

Wings Spread Wide

he awakens
to wistful urgings
to his temptress
her wings spread wide
her neck arched
as if her archer's bow
when he rises
mounts her yearning
her talons dig deep
in clefts of his bowed back
he pokes and prods
her tenderness
his uncommon rod
the fiber of fine oak
worshipping in the sanctity
of her womanhood
corralling her helpless senses
until satisfied by temptation
until broken
until she's broken
and he collapses
upon her plethora of feathers

where soon
he will awaken again
to wistful urgings
to his temptress
her wings spread wide

This The Moving Day

At the close
Of this the moving day
When the rope lines recede
When the processionals fade
The poetry and pageantry
To the annuals of history return
The Bible of Abe Lincoln
The Bible of Martin Luther King Jr
Lay now in state
The National Mall quiet
The symbol of our democracy
Made of stars and stripes
The red stain of blood
White the purity of ideal
Blue the bruises laid bare
Will continue waiving
Waiving in the winds of freedom
Now again
The state of the presidency
Secure
Now again
The perfecting of the Union

Ensuing
At the close
Of this the moving Day

* My inaugural poem written in honor of Barack Obama
  the 44th President of The United States.

ABOUT THE AUTHOR

emmett wheatfall lives in Portland, Oregon where he reads, writes, and performs poetry. He has published three books of poetry entitled *He Sees Things* (2010), *We Think We Know* (2011), and *The Meaning of Me* (2012).

He has published four chapbooks under the titles *Queen of the Nile*, *I Too Am A Slave*, *The Majestic*, and *Midnight In Madrid* through Portland publishing company Naviguer Les Mers Publishing. A number of his poems have been published by online journals and periodicals.

He has released two lyrical poetry CDs. *When I Was Young* (2010) is a highly regarded thematic CD that speaks to love, hope, betrayal, and fidelity addressed in various social and cultural context. *I Loved You Once* (2011) contains great poetry writing set to jazz, blues, and pop musical influences.

emmett has performed lyrical poetry at Jimmy Maks, a premier Northwest Jazz club and one of America's top 100 Jazz clubs. Accompanied by world class Jazz musicians in the persons of Noah Peterson, Gordon Lee, Andre St. James, Edwin Coleman, and Ramsey Embick, he has performed lyrical poetry for sold out audiences.

In addition, he has read and performed lyrical poetry in concert with Oregon Poet Laureate Lawson Inada, and is a participant in the Portland Poetry Slam (PPS) spoken word scene.

emmett is a signed recording artist with Peterson Entertainment, Inc

Printed in the USA
CPSIA information can be obtained
at www.ICGtesting.com
CBHW031109030324
4918CB00010B/430